The Mighty Mekong

Written by Claire Owen

Vietnam

My name is Kim-Ly. I live in Ho Chi Minh City, Vietnam. One of my favorite things to do is take a boat trip on the river with my family. Why are rivers important? How do you think the people who live along the Mekong use the river?

Contents

Wherever you see me, you'll find activities to try and questions to answer.

The Mighty Mekong

The Mekong is the longest river in Southeast Asia. Fed by glaciers in Tibet, the river twists and turns for about 2,600 miles, rushing through gorges in China and flowing through jungles in Laos. It tumbles over waterfalls in Cambodia before reaching the flat Plain of Reeds in southern Vietnam. There, the Mekong fans out in a huge delta before draining into the South China Sea.

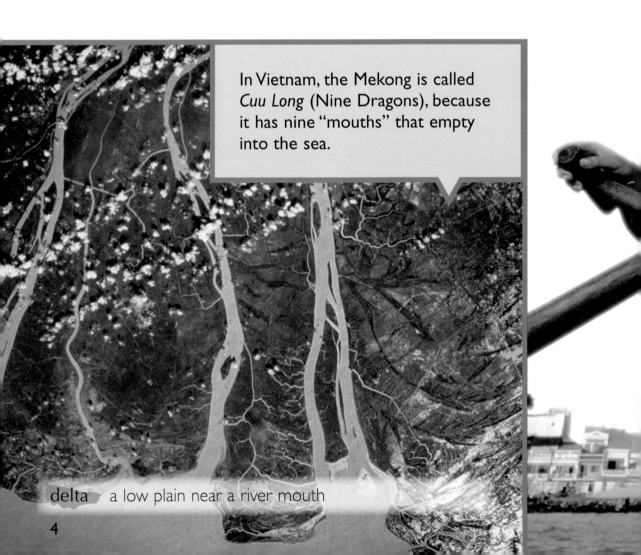

In Vietnam, the Mekong is called *Cuu Long* (Nine Dragons), because it has nine "mouths" that empty into the sea.

delta   a low plain near a river mouth

Tibet

Mekong River

CHINA

MYANMAR

VIETNAM

LAOS

THAILAND

CAMBODIA

Mekong River Delta

Measuring a River

It is a difficult task to measure the length of the Mekong. The river begins high in the remote mountains of Tibet at an altitude of 17,135 feet, and its source was not officially identified until 1999. Furthermore, the Mekong has many tributaries. It has been known to flood to a width of two-and-a-half miles and reach a depth of more than 300 feet. These factors make measuring the river quite a challenge.

The Longest River on Each Continent			
Continent	River	Length (Miles)	Average Discharge (Cubic Feet of Water Per Second)
Africa	Nile	4,145	180,100
Antarctica	–	–	–
Asia	Yangtze	3,915	1,126,500
Australia	Murray–Darling	2,310	27,100
Europe	Volga	2,290	285,300
South America	Amazon	4,005	7,733,900
North America	Mississippi–Missouri*	3,710	572,100

* In some references, the Mississippi–Missouri is considered to be longer than the Amazon. The stated length of a river depends on how it is measured and which tributaries are included.

tributary   a stream or river that flows into a larger river or lake

The Amazon accounts for about 20 percent of all the fresh water that is discharged into the world's oceans. Even 200 miles beyond the mouth of the Amazon, the seawater is fresh enough to drink!

In this photo taken from space, the fresh water discharged from the Amazon can be seen as a brown area.

Figure It Out

1. Compare the length of the Mekong (page 4) and the rivers on page 6. About how much longer or shorter is the Mekong than each of the other rivers?

2. List the rivers from the chart on page 6—

   a. in order of length, from longest to shortest.

   b. in order of discharge, from greatest volume to least volume.

3. On average, how many cubic feet of water does the Nile discharge into the sea—

   a. each minute?

   b. each hour?

   c. each day?

4. How much more water does the Amazon discharge each second than all of the other rivers in the chart combined?

Up the River

In 1866, French explorers traveled up the Mekong in narrow dugout canoes that were pushed forward with bamboo poles. They hoped that the river would turn out to be a profitable trade route to China. However, near the border of Laos and Cambodia, their hopes were dashed when they came to the Khone Falls, a stretch of rapids and waterfalls 6.7 miles long. The explorers also encountered leeches, tigers, quicksand, and diseases!

Khone Falls

quicksand   loose, wet sand that sucks in anything resting on it

Leeches live in jungles and in the shallows of streams, rivers, and lakes. They use disk-shaped suckers to attach themselves to a person's skin and suck blood from their victim.

An artist traveling with the French expedition recorded some of the sights along the way. This drawing shows a dugout canoe (foreground) on the Mekong.

How many years have passed since the French expedition up the Mekong?

Giants of the Mekong

As the longest river in Southeast Asia, the Mekong is an important source of water for six countries. About 90 million people rely on the Mekong in some way, and fishing is a very important industry. The river is home to approximately 240 species of fish, and one-fourth of those species are found only in the Mekong. The largest endemic fish is the Mekong giant catfish.

The Mekong giant catfish is the world's largest freshwater fish without scales. Known in Thailand as *Pla Buk* (Huge Fish), the catfish can grow nearly 10 feet long and weigh as much as 650 pounds. Today, this giant fish is critically endangered.

endemic   native to a particular place and found only there

Other huge fish that live in the Mekong are the giant Siamese carp and the giant freshwater stingray. The carp at the left weighed about 200 pounds. The stingray below was almost 14 feet long and was estimated to weigh about 1,000 pounds.

In central Cambodia, the average person eats $2\frac{3}{4}$ pounds of fish each week. About how many people would a 650-pound catfish feed for a week?

The Rice Basket

Another important industry that relies on the waters of the Mekong is rice farming. Vietnam is one of the world's largest exporters of rice, and more than half of the country's rice crop is grown in the Mekong delta. In 2004, Vietnam produced more than 33 million tons of rice. Most rice is grown on small family farms, and more than half of the Vietnamese work force is engaged in agriculture.

Did You Know?

- In 2004, the world's total rice harvest was a near-record 611 million tons.
- Asian farmers grow about 90 percent of all the world's rice.

The Mekong delta is one of two "rice baskets" in Vietnam. The other important rice-growing area is the delta of the Hong (Red) River.

Use a calculator to figure out each of the missing amounts in the chart below.

Rice Exports from Vietnam

Year	Exports (Tons)	Total Value	Average Price (Per Ton)
2000	3,393,800	$615,829,670	$181.45
2001	3,536,919	$544,982,188	?
2002	3,258,514	?	$184.27
2003	?	$675,818,100	$174.63

An Ancient Grain

Rice originated in Asia thousands of years ago. Fossil remains from rice plants found in a cave in Thailand date back to 10,000 B.C., and humans have been known to cultivate rice for more than 8,000 years. The earliest varieties of rice grew only in warm, damp places. Today, however, there are approximately 7,000 varieties, which suit many different climates. Rice is grown on every continent except Antarctica.

Did You Know?

- In some Asian languages, the words for *rice* and *food* are the same.

- For two billion people in the world, rice makes up at least 50 percent of their diet.

cultivate   to grow from seeds or other plant parts

The Mekong delta is an ideal area for growing floating rice. The rice is planted at the start of the wet season, and the stalks grow rapidly as the floodwaters gradually rise. After several months, the waters recede, and the plants collapse before they are harvested.

Look at these graphs for Can Tho, the main city of the Mekong delta. Which month is the hottest? ... the wettest? Which of the rainy months is the coolest?

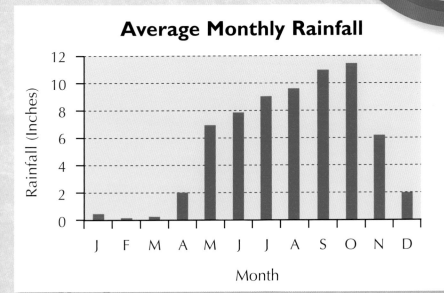

Average Monthly Rainfall

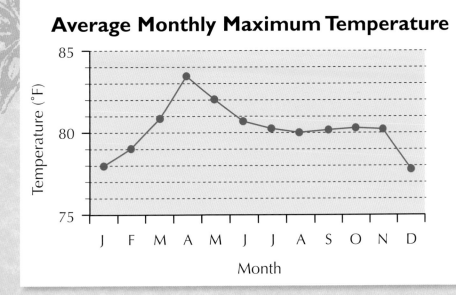

Average Monthly Maximum Temperature

Increasing the Yield

Farmers in the Mekong delta used to grow one rice crop each year. They sowed the seed in July and harvested the crop six months later. Each acre of land produced about 0.4 tons of grain. However, since the 1980s, higher-yielding varieties of rice have been introduced. Some varieties ripen early or can be grown during the winter. This has made it possible for farmers to grow three rice crops each year.

Find the total amount of rice harvested in Vietnam in each of the years below.

Vietnam's Rice Harvests
(Millions of Tons)

Season	2002	2003	2004
Rainy Season	8.130	8.116	7.844
Winter–Spring	15.591	15.600	15.764
Summer–Fall	8.251	8.605	9.676

Make a Multiple-Bar Graph

To make a bar graph that shows Vietnam's rice harvest,
you will need chart paper, a copy of the Blackline Master,
a metric ruler, and three different-colored markers or pencils.

1. Copy the chart shown on page 16, but round each of the numbers to one decimal place.

Vietnam's Rice Harvests
(Millions of Tons)

Season	2002	2003	2004
Rainy Season	8.1	8.1	7.8
Winter–Spring			
Summer–Fall			

2. On the Blackline Master, color a bar 8.1 cm high to show the 2002 Rainy Season harvest.

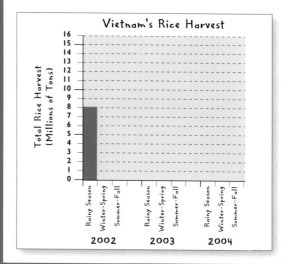

3. Draw bars of the same color to show the Rainy Season harvest for the other two years.

4. Use a different marker to draw the bars for the Winter–Spring harvest. Then use a third color for the Summer–Fall harvest.

Delta Ducks

Of the nearly 30 million ducks that are raised in Vietnam each year, about two-thirds are bred in the Mekong delta. Traditionally, ducks live in the rice paddies, where they eat insects and weeds and eliminate the need for expensive pesticides and herbicides. Additionally, duck manure provides valuable nutrients for the growing rice plants. Some farmers also raise fish in their rice fields.

eliminate to get rid of

The Mighty Mekong

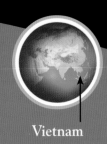

Vietnam

Written by Claire Owen

WorldScapes®: The Mighty Mekong

Product number: ETA 405281
ISBN: 978-0-7406-4295-1

Published in the United States by
ETA/Cuisenaire®
500 Greenview Court
Vernon Hills
IL 60061-1862

Author: Claire Owen
Photo Researcher: Sarah Matthewson
Editor: Frances Bacon
Designer: Avon Willis

Photographs by: Australian Agency for International Development: AusAid, Sept. 2004
(bridge lit by fireworks, p. 21); Hans Kempf, July 2000 (people on bridge, p. 21); **FLPA:**
Mammal Fund Earthviews (p. 22); **Getty Images** (p. 4; leeches, p. 9); **Zeb Hogan**
(pp. 10–11); **Stock Image Group** (person rowing, pp. 4–5); **Tranz:** Corbis (cover; title page;
girl, p. 2, p. 24; farmer planting seeds, pp. 2–3; pp. 7–8; pp. 12–14; p. 16; pp. 18–20; p. 23);
White Lotus Press, Bangkok: www.whitelotusbooks.com (Mekong river scene, p. 9)

The publisher would like to thank Chris Hayes-Kossman, of AusAid (http://photolibrary.
ausaid.gov.au/Cumulus/Standard/index.jsp), for his assistance with the photos on page 21.

11 12 13 14
11 10 9 8 7

Printed in China through Colorcraft Ltd., Hong Kong

800-445-5985
www.etacuisenaire.com

Different varieties of ducks are raised for meat and eggs. Meat birds are larger than layer birds. Each layer produces, on average, about 180 eggs per year. The eggs weigh about 2 ounces each.

About how many eggs will a layer have produced by the time it is 4 years old? Together, how many pounds would all those eggs weigh?

Friendship Bridges

The Mekong flows through six countries, but the river has sometimes separated the people in those countries. In some places, crossing the mighty Mekong by ferry takes an hour or more! In 1994, the Australian government helped build the first Friendship Bridge, which spans the Mekong River between Laos and Thailand. Since then, other countries have helped build bridges in Cambodia and Vietnam.

The first Friendship Bridge, which links Laos and Thailand, is 3,851 feet long and cost $42 million to build.

span   to stretch or reach across

The first bridge across the Mekong delta was opened in the year 2000. The My Thuan Friendship Bridge is 2,165 feet long and cost $95 million to build. Nearly 60,000 people travel by vehicle across the bridge each day, with many more traveling by foot.

On average, how many days would it take for one million people to cross the My Thuan bridge in vehicles?

What is the difference in length between the two Friendship Bridges pictured? What is the difference in cost?

Cause for Concern

Although the Mekong is a huge and powerful river, it is under threat. As the human population of the area grows, pollution is increasing, and overfishing is becoming a problem. The clearing of land for agriculture is causing soil erosion, and dams are altering the river's natural flood cycle. Consequently, there is an urgent need to manage resources in a sustainable way, so that the Mekong will continue to be a mighty river.

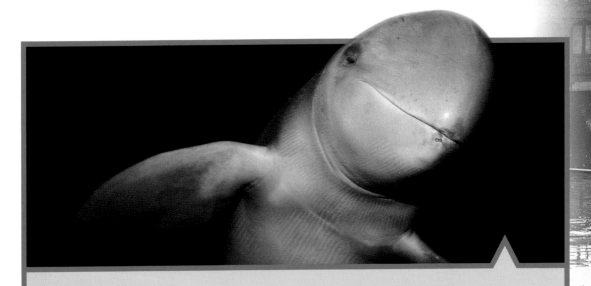

The Mekong was once home to thousands of Irrawaddy dolphins. In the past, some dolphins helped fishermen by driving fish into their throw nets. Today, however, many fishermen use gill nets anchored to the river bed. Dolphins get tangled in these nets and drown. Today, there are only about 100 Irrawaddy dolphins left in the Mekong.

sustainable   able to be kept going over time

These houses on the edge of the Mekong are under threat from erosion of the river bank.

Several large dams, such as this one in China, have been built across the Mekong River, and more dams are planned. Dams are a good way to generate electricity and to prevent catastrophic floods. However, dams stop fish from migrating up the river to breed.

catastrophe   a sudden event that causes great loss, suffering, or damage

Sample Answers

Find out some facts and figures about a river that flows through your city, state, or country.

Page 7
1. 1,545 miles (S)
    1,315 miles (S)
    290 miles (L)   310 miles (L)
    1,405 miles (S)   1,110 miles (S)
    (S = Shorter, L = Longer)

3. a. 10,806,000   b. 648,360,000
    c. 15,560,640,000

4. 5,542,800 cubic feet

Page 11   236 people

Page 13   2001: $154.08
                 2002: $600,446,375
                 2003: 3,870,000

Page 15   April, October, August

Page 19   720 eggs, 90 pounds

Page 21   about 17 days; 1,686 feet; $53 million

Index